THE GREAT ARTISTS
& THEIR WORLD
RENOIR

NEW
FOREST
PRESS

Publisher: Melissa Fairley
Editor: Guy Croton
Designer: Carol Davis
Production Controller: Ed Green
Production Manager: Suzy Kelly

ISBN: 978-1-84898-317-5
Library of Congress Control Number: 2010925218
Tracking number: nfp0004

North American edition copyright © TickTock Entertainment Ltd. 2010
First published in North America in 2010 by New Forest Press,
PO Box 784, Mankato, MN 56002
www.newforestpress.com

Printed in the USA
9 8 7 6 5 4 3 2 1

CONTENTS

INTRODUCTION

One of the main artists associated with the development of the Impressionist movement and one of the best-loved, Pierre-Auguste Renoir became known for his paintings of beautiful women, children, flowers, and surroundings. Over the course of his career, he created some of the most charming examples of Impressionist art, frequently capturing fleeting moments that are like snapshots in paint, filled with sparkling color and light.

CHANGE IN DIRECTION

Although he worked with the Impressionists and exhibited with them, by the early 1880s, Renoir began to follow a new direction. He was always more traditional than the other Impressionists and he became inspired once more by the paintings of the Old Masters who had been a great influence on him when he first decided to become an artist. As a result, his work became more precise, detailed, and structured, with smooth brushstrokes and cooler colors. He later called this his *"manière aigre"* (dry or sour manner) but by the 1890s, he developed another method, blending his Impressionist style with his manière aigre, softening his outlines with small brush marks and using warmer, glowing colors. At the same time he turned from contemporary themes to more timeless subjects, including plump female figures, and mythological stories.

From the age of thirteen, he had been an apprentice as a painter of porcelain in a Parisian factory. He was so skilful at the job that he was nicknamed "Monsieur Rubens." At the porcelain factory, he learned to apply light, fresh colors delicately, and gained an understanding of decoration that later featured in his Impressionist work.

EARLY INFLUENCES

While he had worked in the factory, Renoir often visited the Louvre and admired the work of past artists, particularly the great eighteenth century painters, Watteau, Boucher, and Fragonard as well as the dramatic and colorful canvases of Delacroix. In 1862 he entered the studio of Charles Gleyre where he made friends with Monet, Sisley, and Bazille, who later introduced him to Pissarro, Cézanne, Degas, and Manet. Gleyre taught art conventionally, but also recommended painting and sketching "en plein air" or out of doors, which was quite daring at the time. Many artists sketched outside, but most painted their final, detailed work in their studios. Renoir and a group of his new friends followed the ideas of some landscape painters that were breaking new ground by painting in the Forest of Fontainebleau, about forty miles south of Paris. The idea was not to try to make something perfect as conventional artists did, but to portray just what they saw in front of them. To traditional artists and critics, these sketchy paintings seemed like preparatory work for more detailed pictures produced later in the studio, but to Renoir and his friends, this was finished art.

In the Forest of Fontainebleau, Renoir lightened his palette to include the brighter colors he had enjoyed working with as a porcelain painter. By 1864, he began exhibiting at the official annual art exhibition in Paris, the Salon, but recognition of his work did not come for some time and like several of the other Impressionists, he suffered financial hardship for years. In 1869, he and Monet painted together by the River Seine, capturing the effects of light and air with small marks of brilliant colors. Working quickly to catch the colors in nature before the light changed, the two artists made little attempt to blend their paints or to disguise their brush marks as in conventional painting. These works are considered to be the earliest examples of Impressionism, even though the name had not yet been thought of. Renoir participated in four of the eight Impressionist exhibitions and experimented with various styles and techniques during that time, sometimes applying paint thickly and sometimes building up strong tonal contrasts. Always interested in people, he painted portraits, dancers, the theater, and his friends socializing, as well as flowers and landscapes.

PAINFUL LAST YEARS

In 1892 Renoir began to suffer from rheumatoid-arthritis and by 1912 he was confined to a wheelchair. Nevertheless, he continued to paint until the end of his life, and in his last years he also took up sculpture, directing two young assistants to either place his paintbrush in his hands or to sculpt under his instruction.

THE WORLD OF RENOIR

Pierre Auguste Renoir was born in Limoges, France, on February 25, 1841. His father, Leonard Renoir, was a tailor; his mother, Marguerite Merlet, a dressmaker. The family moved to the Louvre area of Paris when Pierre was just four years old, making home at 23 rue d'Argenteuil. Leonard, Marguerite, and their five children shared the Paris apartment which Renoir later recalled as the size of a "pocket handkerchief." Leonard continued his business as a tailor from the Rue d'Argenteuil apartment, his tailor's bench being transformed into his own bed at night. Renoir was the second youngest so gradually, as his elder brothers Henri and Victor found jobs and moved out of the family home, the pressure on space eased. The family lived in the very center of Paris and could observe from their windows the riots of 1848, which led to the Revolution, which in turn installed Louis Napoleon Bonaparte as President of the Republic of France, and then Emperor. Renoir grew up in a city being transformed by revolutions of state, industry, and, most importantly of all, culture.

Detail showing Renoir's portrait.

PORTRAIT OF 43 PAINTERS
IN THE STUDIO OF GLEYRE, *c.*1862

In 1862, at the age of 21, Renoir was accepted at the École des Beaux-Arts to study art. He was an average pupil, frustrated, as many of the students were, by the unadventurous traditional teaching methods with their dependence on studies from models of antiquity. From 1861, Renoir had attended classes in the private studio of the Swiss painter, Charles Gleyre. Many young hopefuls were attracted to Gleyre's style of teaching, which was far more liberal than the established schools, despite the fact that Gleyre's own painting did not manage to raise itself above the average. Renoir's fellow pupils included Claude Monet, Alfred Sisley, and the talented Frédéric Bazille who was tragically to die in the Franco-Prussian war. This group portrait picture of 43 painters in Gleyre's studio includes a portrait of Renoir, painted by his friend Emile-Henri Laporte.

BATHERS IN THE SEINE (LA GRENOUILLÈRE), 1869

This painting by Renoir is one of four he made of the subject. He painted the scene en plein-air (outdoors) on site. Claude Monet was another painter of the time who went to La Grenouillère to paint. Monet described his plans in a letter to Bazille: *"I have a dream, a picture, the bathers at La Grenouillère. I have done some poor sketches for it, but it is only a dream. Renoir, who has just spent two months here, also wants to paint this motif."*

THE ISLAND BAL DE LA GRENOUILLÈRE

The bathing pools at La Grenouillère, just 20 minutes by train from the central Paris station of Saint-Lazare, were a popular day trip destination for Parisians relaxing on weekends or holidays. Although La Grenouillère translates as "frog-pond" the name had nothing to do with amphibians. "Frogs" was the name given by men to the girls who spent the summers at the pools and who had a reputation for being flirtatious. Renoir described the "frogs" as being: *"very good sorts,"* and found several models who would pose for him among the bathers at La Grenouillère.

THE PORCELAIN PAINTER

At the age of 13 Renoir was apprenticed to a porcelain painter who decorated vases and plates. His brother, Henri, was already established as an engraver and Renoir's family encouraged their children in their artistic trades, eager no doubt to see some money coming in to the family home. Renoir experimented with decorative painting on fans and furniture, as well as porcelain. This vase, painted by Renoir when he was an apprentice, is decorated with figures based on Jean Goujon's *Nymphs*.

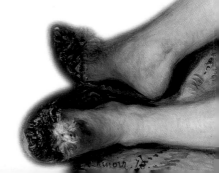

INFLUENCES & EARLY WORKS: ROMANCE & REALISM

PORTRAIT OF ROMAINE LACAUX *(detail),* 1864

This portrait of the daughter of a porcelain manufacturer is one of Renoir's earliest commissioned paintings, as well as one of his most accomplished. Painted when he was only 24 years old, Renoir has managed to capture the freshness of youth and clear-eyed innocence of the young Romaine.

Renoir's grounding in painting began as a commercial artist, painting figures and scenes on porcelain until this craft was made redundant by the introduction of machine printing. This early experience of copying classical figures and rococo scenes helped Renoir acquire skills that he retained all his working life, as well as developing a lasting interest in the work of the classical masters. His early career as a painter, however, began with his studentship under Charles Gleyre, and continued with his admiration of the works of 19th century French artists Eugène Delacroix and Gustave Courbet. In 1848, Courbet had caused a stir in the art world with his realistic paintings depicting simple everyday scenes, such as peasants breaking stones for road mending. This realism reflected Courbet's view of the world and art's place within it, and was a break from the traditional subjects thought suitable for art, such as scenes from antiquity painted in a formal classical style. Courbet's break with convention made it possible for artists such as Édouard Manet to concentrate on realistic scenes, and began to free artists from the tyranny of tradition.

WOMEN OF ALGIERS

Eugène Delacroix

Delacroix was considered a great artist even in his own time. His painting was very influential during the first half of the 19th century. He was a champion of Romantic art which represented uncontrolled nature, including "human nature" or actions, as opposed to the tradition of classicism, which represented fixed ideas of behavior and standards of beauty. Romanticism was therefore considered "modern" and attracted modern-thinking artists. Romantic art sometimes looked toward Oriental subject matter, which was considered exotic and exciting.

THE STONE-BREAKERS

Gustave Courbet

Courbet believed that artists should only paint *"real and existing things."* It led to the conclusion that artists should only believe what they could see with their own eyes. This meant painting the people and scenes they could see around them exactly as they appeared, not how they were taught to imagine they should be. Ordinary people in modern dress became the subject matter, and light and its impression on the scene became important. What better way to get closer to the "truth" than to take the easel and painting to the subject rather than bring the subject to the studio?

WOMAN OF ALGIERS *(detail)*

In 1870, Renoir painted this portrait of a woman of Algiers, heavily influenced by the oriental style that was fashionable at the time. It owes much to Delacroix's painting of the same subject, but Renoir's painting has made the transition from an imaginary scene to a very real one. Delacroix's paintings were dominated by Romantic notions of exoticism relying on imaginary far away places. Renoir's *Woman of Algiers*, dressed in an exotic and colorful costume, is depicted as a very real woman. The model was actually Renoir's 19 year old girlfriend, Lise Trehot, who directly engages the viewer's gaze in a very sensual way. By placing her in an Oriental costume rather than contemporary French dress, Renoir does not offend his viewer's idea of how women should behave.

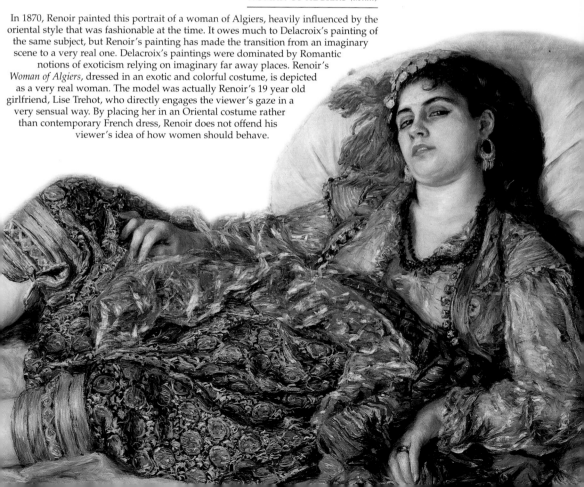

INFLUENCES & EARLY WORKS: IMPRESSIONISM

Renoir's fellow pupils at Charles Gleyre's studio, Monet, Bazille, and Sisley, all continued to work together after Gleyre's retirement in 1864. Monet persuaded them to travel to Fontainebleau to paint directly from nature. Renoir's first submission to the official Paris Salon annual exhibition of painting in 1864, was entitled *Esmeralda Dancing with a Goat*. The acceptance of the picture suggests that it was painted in a more traditional style, as the work of the Realists and Impressionists were continually rejected by the Salon. No record exists of this painting because Renoir later destroyed it on the grounds that it contained asphalt and would not last, although possibly it was because he was not content with the way it appeared. Renoir and his fellow painters had set about painting the world around them—the Paris street scenes, local bathing spots, boating on the river Seine, and scenes from the cafés and music halls. In 1874, the Société Anonyme des Artistes formed to exhibit their pictures, independent from the official Salon. The first exhibition contained works by Monet, Morisot, Renoir, Degas, Cézanne, Pissarro, and Sisley; this group became known as the Impressionists.

THE POPPY FIELD AT ARGENTEUIL

Claude Monet

This picture was painted by Monet in 1873, the year before the first Impressionist exhibition. It shows two pairs of figures walking through a poppy field near his home at Argenteuil on a warm summer's day, and has become one of Impressionism's best-known images. Renoir visited Monet at Argenteuil and they went out into the surrounding countryside to paint. Monet and Renoir shared lodgings together when they were young and poor. Renoir later explained that they spent all their money on studio rent, models, and coal for the stove to keep the models warm. They would time their cooking with their painting so the hot stove both warmed the models and cooked the food.

COUNTRY FOOTPATH IN THE SUMMER, 1874

This picture of figures walking along a country footpath painted in 1874, is full
of the sunlight which filled Monet's landscapes. The scene is remarkably similar
to Monet's painting of the Argenteuil poppy fields and shows Renoir as a true
adherent to Impressionist painting at that time. When the Impressionists mounted their
second exhibition in 1876, at Durand-Ruel's gallery in the rue le Peletier, Renoir was
represented by 15 pictures. Although Impressionism still had its critics Renoir
managed to sell six pictures and was finding admirers such as the publisher Georges
Charpentier, who commissioned
him to paint a family portrait.
This relative success enabled
Renoir to rent a house and
gave him a degree of stability
which allowed him to
concentrate on his art.

LISE *(detail)*, 1868

Renoir had some early successes
with paintings being accepted
by the official Salon in the 1860s,
such as this portrait of Lise. This
painting of his girlfriend Lise Trehot
was unusual in that it was full
length, a convention normally
reserved for royalty. Artist and
critic Zacharie Astruc described
Lise, as: *"the daughter of the people,
with all her typical Parisian features."* One
reaction to the picture was: *"The whole thing
is so natural and has been observed so accurately
that it will appear wrong... we are used to
imagining nature in terms of conventional
colors."* The painting was purchased by
the writer Theodore Duret for 1,200 francs.

THE ART OF HIS DAY

Renoir's career as a painter developed alongside the Impressionists, who are so well known today. Their depictions of comfortable middle-class scenes either in the Parisian streets or surrounding countryside, differed from the earlier Realist imagery such as Millet's peasant scenes, but nevertheless sought to paint pictures of real life as they experienced it. Many of Renoir's contemporaries, however, continued to paint in the traditional way, depicting religious or mythological scenes in a highly finished style. These artists found continued acceptance at the official Salon where their paintings were exhibited. The Impressionists' paintings with their sketchy unfinished style and modern subject matter were considered too shocking to be exhibited at the Salon, where the unsuspecting French public might see them. The technology of the day also had an impact on the development of Impressionism. The growing number of newspapers and journals circulated wider and wider, thanks to more efficient and cheaper reproduction methods, and an increasingly literate public were able to read about the latest art, and see reproductions. The movement even owed its name to a journalist. A review by critic Louis Léroy referred to the "Exhibition of Impressionists" in the magazine *Le Charivari*.

THE GULF OF MARSEILLES

Paul Cézanne

Paul Cézanne was the son of a hat-maker who moved into banking and became a wealthy citizen of his home town of Aix-en-Provence. Cézanne studied art in Paris, where he met Pissarro and the circle of Impressionist painters with whom he exhibited in 1874. He met and fell in love with artist's model, Hortense Fiquet, in Paris and they had an illegitimate son whose existence Cézanne kept from his parents. When they discovered the truth they halved his allowance leaving the family to borrow money where they could. When Cézanne inherited his father's fortune he concentrated on painting in Provence, concerning himself with form and space, making "something solid" of Impressionism.

LE PONT DE L'EUROPE

Gustave Caillebotte

Gustave Caillebotte was a wealthy collector of Impressionist paintings and a talented artist in his own right. His work was not considered to be as important as the Impressionists, but in the 1960s his art was "rediscovered" and is now very popular. Caillebotte painted domestic everyday scenes of Paris life using dramatic perspective and a more highly finished technique than his Impressionist friends. There is an overwhelming sense of modernism in his paintings, stressed by the open air "snapshot" feeling, as if the image has been captured through the lens of a camera. His paintings were respected by his friends and contemporaries and were exhibited at the Impressionist exhibition of 1876. Caillebotte built up a large collection of Impressionist paintings including ten by Renoir, often buying them from friends at inflated prices in order to support them. In his will he left his collection to the State, on the condition that they be exhibited at the Louvre. When he died in 1894, the more conservative artists protested that if the State accepted his collection it would be a sign of moral decline and the end of the nation. Eventually 38 of the 57 paintings were exhibited, supposedly on the grounds of a lack of space at the Louvre.

THE LIFE OF RENOIR

~1841~
Born on February 25 at Limoges, France

~1844~
Renoir family move to Paris

~1854~
Renoir becomes an apprentice at Levy Brothers, painting plates and vases

~1858~
Made redundant by new technique for printing onto porcelain

~1862~
Studies at Charles Gleyre's studio where he meets Sisley, Monet, and Bazille

PORTRAIT OF JULIE MANET

Berthe Morisot

Berthe Morisot's truly Impressionist paintings of elegant Parisian women are notable for their freshness and delicacy. Morisot was able to paint the crisp starched linen and soft silk of evening dress with blurred brushstrokes, which are dragged across the surface of the canvas retaining their immediacy of touch. The "impression" of having captured the fleeting moment as a woman prepares to dress for the evening or, interrupted, glances toward the viewer, makes her a true Impressionist. Morisot married Édouard Manet's brother, Eugene, and they had a daughter, Julie, who appears in a number of the Impressionist group's paintings including those by Renoir.

THE LIFE OF RENOIR

~1864~
Has a painting
accepted by the Salon
but later destroys it

~1865~
Meets Lise Trehot who
becomes his girlfriend
and model

~1872~
Has two paintings purchased
by dealer Durand-Ruel and
spends the summer painting
with Monet

~1874~
Exhibits at the first
Impressionist show

~1880~
Meets Aline Charigot

~1881~
Travels to
Algeria, Venice,
Rome, and Naples

~1883~
Experiments with
new "Dry Style"
of painting

~1885~
Birth of his son Pierre

~1888~
First attack of rheumatoid
arthritis which leaves his
face partially paralyzed

~1892~
Young Girls at the Piano
purchased by the State

~1894~
Birth of son Jean

~1890~
Marries Aline Charigot

~1901~
Birth of son Claude (Coco)

Renoir's second son, Jean, was born on September 15, 1894. In Jean Renoir's own memoirs of his father he writes that his mother exclaimed on his birth: *"Heavens how ugly, take it away!"* Jean became a famous film director as well as a writer of several books, including a biography of his father. Another witness to Jean's birth was Gabrielle Renard, the 15 year old cousin of Aline Charigot who had come from her home in Essoyes to help with the preparations for the birth. Gabrielle stayed to help look after Jean. She became Renoir's favorite model, at first posing with the children, as in this portrait with Jean. In Renoir's later years she became an important figure in Renoir's exploration of the female form in such paintings as *Gabrielle with Jewel Box* (page 28). Gabrielle continued as Renoir's principal model until 1914, when she married and left the Renoir home in Cagnes.

THE CLOWN

(detail), 1909
Claude Renoir was born in 1901, when Renoir was 60 years old. Claude was only 14 when his mother, Aline, died at the age of 56, after fighting diabetes. Claude, nicknamed Coco, was often a model for Renoir and in this painting the six year old Claude is dressed in a clown's outfit.

FAMILY, FRIENDS, & OTHERS

Renoir did not come from a comfortable middle-class family, as many of his Impressionist friends did. His father's tailoring business was just sufficient to support the family, and Renoir found a job as an apprentice to a porcelain painter when he was 13 to supplement the family income. When he decided to study painting at the studio of Charles Gleyre he soon became friends with Claude Monet, Frédéric Bazille, and Alfred Sisley. He kept company with this artistic circle and had many girlfriends among the models who posed for his paintings, but it was not until Renoir was nearly 40 that he met Aline Charigot, a 19 year old dressmaker who lived near Renoir's home in the rue Saint-Georges. Aline posed for Renoir and fell in love with him, despite her mother's advice to find a man who was old and wealthy. Aline traveled to Italy with Renoir in 1881, and much later referred to the trip as their "honeymoon," despite the fact they were not actually married until 1890.

BUST OF MADAME RENOIR WITH PIERRE

Aline Charigot came from the Burgundy area of France and was teased by her Parisian friends about her accent and country ways. When they first met, Renoir and Aline spent much of their time together by the river Seine, traveling by train from Saint-Lazare to the Chatou bridge, and then the Fournaise restaurant. Renoir's well known painting *Luncheon of the Boating Party* (page 21), depicts a scene at the Fournaise restaurant which shows Aline holding a small dog. Aline moved in with Renoir after his return from a trip to Algeria in 1881. Their first child, Pierre, was born in 1885. Renoir found a studio near the family apartments in the rue Houdon in order that, according to Aline: *"the baby will be able to cry to his heart's content."* Pierre became an actor, but went to fight in World War I where he was badly wounded.

DÉJEUNER A BERNEVAL, c.1905

This is a charming domestic interior scene, at home with the Renoir family.

FAMILY, FRIENDS, & OTHERS

The small group of friends who studied together under Charles Gleyre and then continued to paint together were at the very center of the movement which was subsequently named Impressionism. In 1865, Renoir shared a studio with Alfred Sisley and a year later, after Sisley was married, he moved in with Frédéric Bazille, a talented young painter who was tragically killed at the age of 29, during the Franco-Prussian war. In 1867, Bazille rented a Paris studio at 20 rue Visconti. From here he wrote to his mother: *"Since my last letter there is something new at the rue Visconti. Monet has fallen from the sky with a collection of huge canvases which will be a great success at the World Fair. He will stay here until the end of the month. With Renoir that makes two needy painters that I'm housing. It's a veritable sanatorium. I'm delighted, I have plenty of space, and both are very good company."* Renoir and Bazille continued to be close friends, later moving together to a studio near the famous Café Guerbois which became the meeting place for the new wave of modern-thinking artists, such as Manet, Monet, Degas, and Pissarro, as well as writers like Émile Zola, Edmond Duranty, and Zacharie Astruc.

PORTRAIT OF JULIE MANET *(detail)*, c.1894

Julie Manet often stayed with the Renoir family, particularly after the death of her parents, Berthe Morisot and Eugene Manet, which left her orphaned at the age of 17. Morisot had asked Renoir to look after Julie, although her official guardian was the poet Stéphane Mallarmé.

MADAME ALPHONSE DAUDET *(detail)*, 1875

Alphonse Daudet was a successful novelist and playwright who, together with such writers as Émile Zola, was regarded as one of the leading members of the Realist movement in literature. Daudet was a great supporter of Impressionism, commissioning this portrait of his wife and buying works from a number of other artists. He was a frequent visitor to the Nouvelle-Athènes café, mixing with the artistic set who met to talk about their work. He was also often invited to Renoir's house where he would join the likes of Zola, Odilon Redon, and Stéphane Mallarmé for dinner.

PORTRAIT OF CLAUDE MONET *(detail)*, 1875

Claude Monet moved to Argenteuil, a suburb of Paris, in 1871. Renoir was amongst the many visitors that stayed with Monet at Argenteuil. When they were together Monet persuaded Renoir to take up his easel and go out into the countryside to paint, en plein-air. Several of Renoir's paintings are of views of the Seine such as the picture of racing boats entitled The Seine at Argenteuil. Renoir also made numerous portraits of his friend Claude Monet and Claude's wife Camille. Monet's obsession with capturing in paint the changing moods of his subject matter according to the light, made him the leading exponent of Impressionism. In his own words, Monet wanted to *"ensnare the light, and throw it directly on to the canvas."*

PORTRAIT OF RICHARD WAGNER, 1882

Renoir was introduced to Wagner's music by a friend at a time when national sentiment was against the composer. This made Renoir determined to like his music and Renoir was eventually introduced to Wagner in person, at which time he made three sketches (executed in under an hour), and this portrait. During the meeting, Wagner managed to offend the artist because of his views of French composers who Wagner hated. Renoir expressed his like for the music of Offenbach which Wagner dismissed as *"little music, but not bad."* Later on Renoir attended a performance of Wagner's opéra Die Walküre at Bayreuth, and commented: *"They have no right to shut people up in the dark for three solid hours...you are forced to look at the only place where there is any light; the stage. It's absolute tyranny...We might as well be frank about it; Wagner's music is boring."*

LE MOULIN DE LA GALETTE, 1876

The painting, which has been described as the most beautiful picture of the 19th century, appears at first glance to be chaotic. The foreground and background merge, and the overlapping forms of the figures are often indistinguishable. The sunlight that filters through the foliage casts shadows that fall across the figures and ground alike, creating a dappled effect that unifies the picture.

Renoir made many studies from models for his figures in *Le Moulin de la Galette*. The two young girls in the center of the picture, one resting her arm on the other's shoulder, are Jeanne and Estelle, seamstresses known as "grisettes," dressed in the latest Paris style. Renoir described how he saw Jeanne on the streets of Montmartre, thought her the ideal model, and stopped and spoke to her. *"I don't go in for that sort of thing Monsieur,"* she replied. Renoir noted that: *"She had lovely hands, the ends of her fingers were swollen from being pricked by needles."* Eventually, Renoir persuaded Jeanne's mother to let her daughter pose for him in return for payment, and soon Jeanne's sister Estelle also became Renoir's model.

The pair of dancers depicted center-left is the Cuban painter Pedro Vidal with Margot Legrand. Margot appears to be the same young girl who Jean Renoir recalls was nursed by his father and Dr Gachet, but she died of suspected small-pox three years after this picture was painted.

WHAT DO THE PAINTINGS SAY?
PARIS SOCIETY

The years before the end of the 19th century are known in
France as the Belle Époque, the golden age when life was for
the enjoying. This description does not convey the fact that
it was also the time when many were struggling for equal
rights such as workers and women in general. Nevertheless,
it was a time when Paris prospered with new roads,
railways, and buildings and the middle classes became more
secure and prosperous. Mass entertainment was available in
the form of the café-concerts and dance halls, the most
popular of which was the *Folies-Bergère*, which still exists today. Renoir
painted modern Parisian life; images of young people at play, in the park,
the dance hall, strolling along the boulevards show us the pleasant side of
Paris life. Renoir was aware that he concentrated on the nice things when
he said: *"There are enough unpleasant things in this world. We don't have to
paint them as well."* Although Renoir concentrated on the pleasant side of
life, he painted scenes from the ordinary everyday world of the Parisian
worker at play, not the fashionable well-to-do classes, and it is this record
of real life that makes his painting fascinating.

The pipe smoker
(on the right)
is Norbert Goeneutte,
and seated next to him
with pen poised is
writer Georges Rivière.

DANCING AT THE MOULIN DE LA GALETTE

A building program in the 1860s and 1870s, transformed the landscape
of Paris. Some of the surrounding parishes became part of the city
as it grew and grew. Montmartre had been a village on a hill with
windmills and vineyards before it was swallowed up by Paris. The
fashion for public dances in the 1870s, meant that nearly every
available space in Paris, from bars and courtyards to squares and
parks, were at some time used for this new craze. The best-known
dance-bar in Montmartre was le Moulin de la Galette, or "le Radet"
for short. It had an outdoor dance floor as well as a bar for red wine
and "galettes," a kind of circular waffle from which it gained its name.

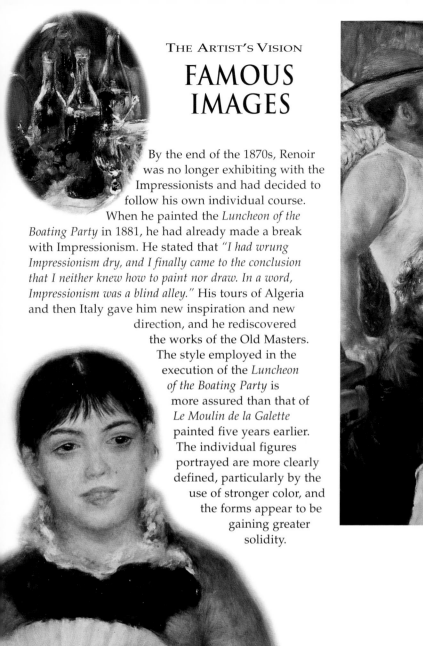

THE ARTIST'S VISION
FAMOUS IMAGES

By the end of the 1870s, Renoir was no longer exhibiting with the Impressionists and had decided to follow his own individual course. When he painted the *Luncheon of the Boating Party* in 1881, he had already made a break with Impressionism. He stated that *"I had wrung Impressionism dry, and I finally came to the conclusion that I neither knew how to paint nor draw. In a word, Impressionism was a blind alley."* His tours of Algeria and then Italy gave him new inspiration and new direction, and he rediscovered the works of the Old Masters. The style employed in the execution of the *Luncheon of the Boating Party* is more assured than that of *Le Moulin de la Galette* painted five years earlier. The individual figures portrayed are more clearly defined, particularly by the use of stronger color, and the forms appear to be gaining greater solidity.

YOUNG WOMAN WITH A FAN (*detail*), 1881

This portrait of Alphonsine, daughter of restaurant owner Alphonse Fournaise, captures the charm which made her a favored model with many male admirers. She features in *Luncheon of the Boating Party*, leaning against the rail.

THE LUNCHEON OF THE BOATING PARTY, 1880/1

The scene depicted in this well-known painting is the Restaurant Fournaise on the Ile de Chatou, a little island in the River Seine near the Ile de Croissy. It was a short train ride from Renoir's studio in the center of Paris. The owner of the restaurant, Alphonse Fournaise, had built a landing stage for the Parisians who wished to swim and hire boats on the river, and he began to serve refreshments on the stage. Renoir recalls the place *"where life was a perpetual holiday and the world knew how to laugh in those days."* Renoir often used to visit the Restaurant Fournaise with his girlfriend Aline.

The figure wearing a top hat and engaged in conversation at the back of the scene is the banker and art collector Charles Ephrussi.

Aline Charigot, Renoir's future wife, sits at the table holding a small dog. Behind is Alphonse Fournaise, the restaurant owner.

In the background is Paul Lhote holding actress Jeanne Samary by the waist.

The seated figure wearing the straw hat is painter Gustave Caillebotte, who talks to actress Ellen Andrée.

RENOIR'S FRIENDS

The painting shows many of Renoir's friends, several of whom sat for Renoir in his studio so he could finish the picture. The group is notable for its social mix, with flower sellers and bankers drinking side by side. The relaxed scene is full of meaningful glances and intimate touches.

THE UMBRELLAS, 1881-6

This painting clearly demonstrates Renoir's different approaches to painting in the 1880s. The artist returned to this painting again and again over a period of years. The figures on the right of the picture are painted in Renoir's "Impressionist" style of the 1870s, with bright colors but soft outlines and loose brushstrokes. The two figures on the left however were painted in a later style which has more clearly defined outlines, a more "finished" surface and more subdued colors.

It is thought that the painting was begun around 1881, because the right-hand figures are wearing dresses and hats that were fashionable at that time, and Renoir normally dressed his models in the latest fashions. By 1883, simpler dresses came into style and the woman holding a basket is dressed in a style which was the height of fashion in 1885, but which had fallen out of fashion by 1887. Recent X-ray examination of the painting suggests that the woman on the left was first painted in the earlier Impressionist method around 1881, with skirts similar to the other women in the picture, complete with white lace cuffs and collar and a hat. This figure was over-painted in about 1885.

DETECTION THROUGH COLOR

Further examination of *The Umbellas* reveals the presence of cobalt blue pigment in the right hand section of the picture, and in the original painting underneath the left-hand figures. This pigment was used by Renoir only during the 1870s and early 1880s. French Ultramarine, a pigment used later by Renoir, was found in the colors on the left-hand figures we see today. He also experimented with removing the oil medium and replacing it with a water-based medium to bind the colors because he thought the oil would eventually darken and spoil his colors, although this experiment was without success. This examination of the use of pigments and medium enables art historians to find out the history of the painting.

22

HOW WERE THEY MADE? THE DRY STYLE

When Renoir visited Italy in 1881, he went to see the art of the great masters such as Michelangelo, Raphael, and Bernini. He later recalled that he became tired of the draped figures with too many folds and muscles, and preferred the Pompeiian frescoes in the Naples Museum. He marveled at the wonderful colors achieved by the fresco painters with such a limited range of colors made from earths and vegetable dyes, and even confessed to repairing a wall painting using paints in powder form that he found in a nearby mason's house. The experience of Renoir's Italian trip was certainly one factor that made him change the way he was painting. By 1883, Renoir openly admitted that Impressionism was a dead end and that he was looking for a new style. He rejected the Impressionist way of painting outdoors, stating that: *"An artist who paints straight from nature is really only looking for nothing but momentary effects. He does not try to be creative himself, and as a result the pictures soon become monotonous."* Renoir's exploration of new ways of painting in the 1880s have now become known as his "Dry Period."

THE SCHOOL OF ATHENS (detail)

Raphael

Renoir's gradual disillusionment with the Impressionist style of rapidly building-up the surface of the canvas with touches of color was hastened by what he saw on his trip to Italy. He admired the purity and grandeur of Raphael's wall paintings, which retained bright colorful surfaces and were masterful compositions with great clarity of structure and form.

WHAT DO THE PAINTINGS SAY? A NEW DIRECTION

Renoir's "Dry Period" is also sometimes known
as his "Ingresque" period after the famous French
painter Jean Ingres. Ingres was a dominant influence
in French painting in the earlier part of the 19th
century. Ingres spent a good part of his career in Italy
and was a devoted follower of the art of Raphael—
the great Italian painter of the High Renaissance.
The art of Ingres, in his admiration of Raphael, was in turn
admired by Renoir. This direct line of influence extends
back to Raphael's source of inspiration; the great classical
art of ancient Greece. In pursuing this new direction
in his painting Renoir was rejecting the
modern art of Impressionism which he felt
had lost its way. He was returning to the
traditional values which had remained
unchanged for centuries. Renoir became
interested in the methods of Renaissance
artists and he criticized the modern
teaching methods which had replaced
the apprenticeship system. The culmination
of his new direction was a large painting
called *The Bathers*.

THE BLONDE BATHER

This painting was made by Renoir in 1887, at the height of his
"Dry Period." The influence of Ingres is quite evident, the
formal pose of the figure against a classical landscape recalling
the fresco paintings Renoir had visited during his trip to Italy.
The painting resembles fresco painting because of its bright
coloring, smooth finish, and clear edges around the female form.
However Renoir does not resist breaking-up the landscape with
individually applied brushstrokes. About this time a critic asked
Renoir whether he considered himself a descendant of Ingres,
to which Renoir replied: *"I only wish I was."*

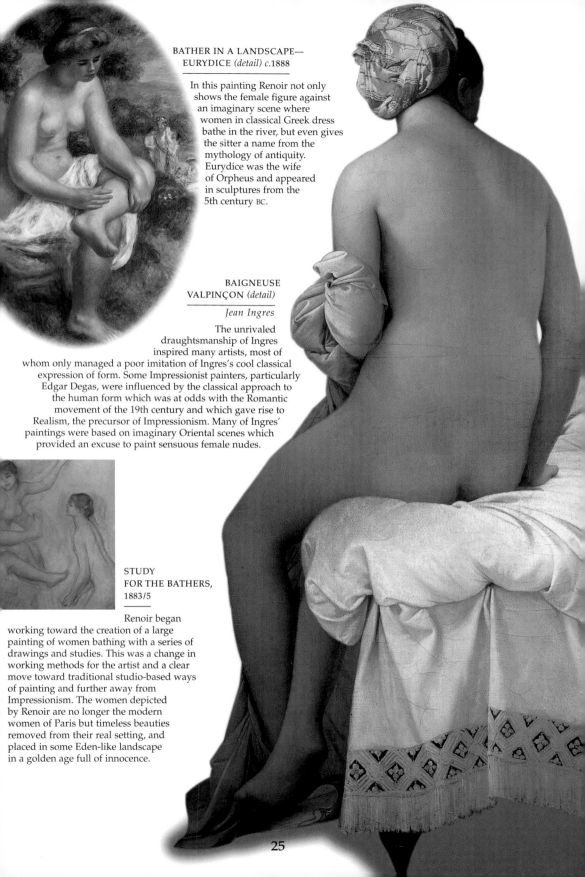

BATHER IN A LANDSCAPE— EURYDICE (detail) c.1888

In this painting Renoir not only shows the female figure against an imaginary scene where women in classical Greek dress bathe in the river, but even gives the sitter a name from the mythology of antiquity. Eurydice was the wife of Orpheus and appeared in sculptures from the 5th century BC.

BAIGNEUSE VALPINÇON (detail)

Jean Ingres

The unrivaled draughtsmanship of Ingres inspired many artists, most of whom only managed a poor imitation of Ingres's cool classical expression of form. Some Impressionist painters, particularly Edgar Degas, were influenced by the classical approach to the human form which was at odds with the Romantic movement of the 19th century and which gave rise to Realism, the precursor of Impressionism. Many of Ingres' paintings were based on imaginary Oriental scenes which provided an excuse to paint sensuous female nudes.

STUDY FOR THE BATHERS, 1883/5

Renoir began working toward the creation of a large painting of women bathing with a series of drawings and studies. This was a change in working methods for the artist and a clear move toward traditional studio-based ways of painting and further away from Impressionism. The women depicted by Renoir are no longer the modern women of Paris but timeless beauties removed from their real setting, and placed in some Eden-like landscape in a golden age full of innocence.

THE GREAT BATHERS—
THE NYMPHS (detail)

Renoir continued the theme of Bathers from the 1880s to the end of his life. This picture was painted about 1918, when Renoir was 77 years old. The figures in the pastoral landscape appear almost to be part of the ground upon which they lie. They have a massiveness and solidity which makes them appear like sculptures modeled out of clay, but are painted in striking flesh tones which are echoed in the grass and the trees which surround them. Renoir was racked by arthritis towards the end of his life and was only able to paint by having his paintbrushes wedged into his bandaged hands. It was in this way that the *Great Bathers* was painted.

THE BATHERS

Renoir exhibited his new paintings at the Georges Petit Gallery. They were exhibited alongside paintings by artists such as Monet, Pissarro, Morisot, and Whistler, and caused something of a stir because of Renoir's departure from Impressionism. The painter Camille Pissarro, a friend of Renoir, wrote to his son: *"Durand has been to Petits; he has seen the Renoirs, and doesn't like his new style— he doesn't like it at all."* Durand-Ruel was an influential dealer who had championed Impressionist art and he was evidently discouraged to find that one of his artists had now adopted a different style of painting. Pissarro commented on Renoir's new style: *"I can quite understand the effort he is making. It is a very good thing not to want to go on repeating oneself, but he has concentrated all his effort on line. The figures stand out against each other without any sort of relationship and the whole thing is meaningless. Renoir is no draughtsman and without the lovely colors he used to use he is incoherent."*

NYMPHS BATHING *François Girardon*

This bas-relief of nymphs bathing by the 17th century artist François Girardon, decorates one of the fountain pools in the park of Versailles. Renoir found it a source of inspiration for his *Bathers* picture as well as other works.

THE BATHERS

This painting was made over a period of several years and finally exhibited at Georges Petit's gallery in 1887. Renoir has created a picture which is completely unlike his former Impressionist works. The subject matter is drawn from a classical source and has none of the spontaneity in execution that typifies Impressionism. In fact the pigment was spread with a knife and smoothed over as much as possible to create a highly finished surface. The idealized beauty of the female forms in their carefully arranged poses have nothing to do with Paris in the 1880s, and are divorced from any real or natural context. The women recall the porcelain decorations that Renoir made in his youth and the only real similarity with his earlier painting is the richness of color, particularly in the surrounding landscape, which typifies Renoir's art.

DIANA BATHING

François Boucher

The Rococo style of the 18th century artist François Boucher was much admired by Renoir. Boucher's paintings of beautiful young women in classical landscapes were an obvious inspiration, as much for the subject matter as the style of painting.

GABRIELLE WITH JEWEL BOX, 1911

This painting made in 1910, shows Renoir's late style. The model is Gabrielle Renard, the young cousin of Renoir's wife Aline. Renoir was quite open about his fascination for women's bodies and talked about them in a way some would find unacceptable today. To the artist they were objects to be observed and depicted: the quality of the skin compared to a fruit which must respond well to the light; the arrangement of the facial features must be in harmony *"with almond shaped eyes, which should be halfway between the top of the head and the tip of the chin."* Some critics think that this is why his models appear to be without spirit—they are painted as if they were fruit or flowers. Renoir's depiction of the female form is without lust. The women appear trance-like, increasingly detached from their surroundings.

BATHER WITH LONG HAIR
(detail), 1910

Renoir concentrated on voluptuous nudes who posed in a sea of vibrant color, and it is almost as if his struggle with arthritis which gave him difficulty holding his paintbrushes allowed him the artistic freedom to relax his style, painting in a freer way with looser, broader brushstrokes. The female figures are as one with the landscape, and no longer appear to be conscious compositions, carefully arranged, but merge effortlessly with the background creating natural and sensuous imagery.

HOW WERE THEY MADE? THE LATE STYLE

In the 1890s Impressionist painting was becoming established in some circles, particularly with some influential collectors, but as a style of painting it was being surpassed by new styles such as the Symbolism of Paul Gauguin. Renoir by this time was an old man who suffered severe attacks of crippling rheumatoid arthritis, which forced him to spend the winter months in the relative warmth of the South of France. Finally in 1905, he moved with his family to Cagnes, a small town near Antibes on the Mediterranean coast. He had a house built which he called "Les Collettes" which was to become his studio until his death. Toward the end of his life his arthritis was so severe that he was permanently wheelchair-bound and his hands became deformed to such an extent that he was unable to hold any object. He continued to paint with brushes wedged into his bandaged hands, and his pictures became more colorful then ever before.

THE JUDGEMENT OF PARIS

Peter Paul Rubens

Renoir's depiction of the female form developed and became more massive, taking on proportions which remind us of the 17th century Dutch artist Rubens, and dominate the picture frame. The figures are completely timeless and might be from classical mythology or from the present day, but are isolated from everything except their landscape. The backgrounds are reduced to a field of color, still Impressionistic in execution, and the whole is soaked in the Mediterranean sunlight which make the colors come alive.

CATHERINE HESSLING IN THE FILM NANA *(right)*

Catherine Hessling (also shown with Renoir in his studio), was a model who worked at the Nice Academie de Peinture and who went to work for Renoir when he was looking for models for his large *Great Bathers* painting. Dédée, as she was then known, traveled by train every day from Nice to Renoir's studio in Cagnes to pose for the artist. After Renoir's death in 1919, his son Jean married Dédée and she became an actress appearing in the early films directed by Jean Renoir, under her stage name Catherine Hessling.

THE AUDIENCE FOR THE PICTURES

Renoir had no means of financial support except from odd jobs or from the sale of his paintings. At the beginning of his career as an artist, times were hard. The society formed by the Impressionist group in 1873, with Renoir a member, had to be dissolved in 1875 due to large debts and the artists were forced to sell their pictures. They were auctioned at the Hotel Drouot in Paris on March 24, 1875, with disastrous results. With a hostile crowd and few buyers, Renoir sold 20 canvases for 2,000 francs compared to the 200,000 francs a respected Salon artist could earn for one painting alone. Early on, Renoir depended on friends to purchase paintings, receiving support from Édouard Manet, Victor Chocquet, and others. Chocquet was a civil servant in the Ministry of Finance who could ill afford to buy paintings. Renoir is reported to have said of him: *"What a charming crackpot... he scraped up the means to buy paintings from his salary... and never gave a thought to whether or not the art would appreciate in value."*

PORTRAIT OF
DELPHINE LEGRAND (*detail*), 1878

Some of the most charming of all Renoir's work are his portraits of children. In this picture of Delphine Legrand, daughter of friend and art dealer Alphonse Legrand, Renoir is able to create a sense of innocence and vulnerability which captures the spirit of the sitter.

MONSIEUR AND MADAME BERNHEIM, 1910

The Bernheim family were art dealers who actively
supported the Impressionist painters. The
Bernheims organized an important exhibition for
Renoir in 1900, and continued to represent his
work up to and beyond Renoir's death. During
this time Renoir made several portraits of the
Bernheim family members including this picture of
Berheim-Jeune and his wife. The family was very
rich, with a magnificent chateau, a house in Paris,
a dozen motorcars, and even an airship. Most
importantly to Renoir, however, was that they had
"beautiful wives whose skins took to the light."

MADAME CHARPENTIER *(detail)*

In 1876, Renoir painted this portrait
of Marguerite Charpentier, wife of
Georges Charpentier, the publisher
of famous novelists such as Flaubert,
Zola, and Maupassant. The family
were very wealthy and had a
reputation for gathering together
the most interesting people of the
day; writers, painters, composers, as
well as actresses, and popular singers.
The Charpentiers supported Renoir as they
did other artists, commissioning portraits of
the family and using their influence to ensure
his paintings were exhibited, thereby giving
Renoir a degree of financial security. Renoir noted
of the sessions with Marguerite Charpentier:
*"She reminds me of the sweethearts of my youth, the
models of Fragonard. The two daughters had lovely dimples. I was
congratulated. I forgot the attacks of the newspapers. I had models
who were willing to sit for free and who were full of goodwill."*

PINK AND BLUE, 1881

Alice and Elizabeth Cahen
d'Anvers were daughters of
a wealthy banker. Renoir was
commissioned to paint several
portraits of the two girls after
Charles Ephrussi, owner of
the *Gazette des Beaux-Arts*
had introduced Renoir to the
Cahen family. It appears that
the Cahens were disappointed
with the double portrait and
decided to hang it in the servants
quarters, out of view of their friends.

WHAT THE CRITICS SAY

NUDE IN THE SUNLIGHT, 1876

In 1876, Durand-Ruel exhibited Renoir's paintings at the rue le Pelletier, including *Nude in the Sunlight*. The art critic Albert Wolff wrote in *Le Figaro*: "*Try and explain to Monsieur Renoir that a woman's torso is not a mass of rotting flesh, with violet-toned green spots all over it, indicating a corpse in the final stages of decay... And this collection of vulgarities has been exhibited in public without a thought for possible fatal consequences. Only yesterday a poor man was arrested in the rue le Pelletier, after leaving the exhibition, because he began biting everyone in sight.*"

Renoir's art has justifiably taken its place among the great Impressionist works, and he is considered today to be one of the small group who changed the course of art in the latter half of the 19th century. Like his contemporary painters he found acceptance slow during his working life, but toward the end of his career gained recognition, fame, and the money that came with it. Renoir never had any pretensions about his art; he wanted to paint what he found attractive and amusing, and by his own admission did not dwell on any concern to express great ideas or emotions. He hated any notion of artists being more than simple laborers who day after day had a job to do—paint. This may be because of his relatively humble beginnings, but whatever the reason, critics and especially art historians, in the 20th century have regarded his art as somehow slighter, less important than his contemporaries. By contrast the non-specialist public at large have always found his art attractive, accessible, and enjoyable.

PORTRAIT OF A YOUNG GIRL *(detail)*, 1888

Renoir's habit of making the eyes of his portrait subjects dark in contrast to the surrounding pale face, attracted the attention of Arthur Baignieres, who wrote of Renoir's painting *Mother and Children* in 1874:"*From afar we see a bluish haze, from which six chocolate drops forcefully emerge. Whatever could it be? We come closer; the sweets are the eyes of three people and the haze a mother and her daughters.*"

YOUNG GIRLS AT THE PIANO, 1892

In 1892, the poet Stéphane Mallarmé and the art critic Claude Roger-Marx persuaded Henri Roujon, the Director of the Beaux-Arts, to purchase a Renoir painting for the State collection. An informal commission resulted in Renoir painting five versions of *Young Girls at the Piano*. The State purchased one of the pictures on May 2, 1892, for the sum of 4,000 francs. The State had only acquired paintings by one other of the original Impressionist group, Alfred Sisley. Mallarmé stated his support for Renoir in a letter to Roujon: *"It is my feeling, as well as the agreed opinion of everyone else, that you cannot be sufficiently congratulated on having chosen such a definitive, refreshing, bold work of maturity for a museum."* Two years earlier Renoir's friends had asked on his behalf for him to be decorated by the State for his work as a painter, but Renoir refused the honor.

NEWS OF THE DIFFERENT EXHIBITIONS

There is an exhibition of the INTRANSIGENTS (Impressionists) in the Boulevard des Capucines, or rather, you might say, of the LUNATICS, of which I have already given you a report. If you would like to be amused, and have a little time to spare, don't miss it.

At the time of the first Impressionist exhibitions the press were very hostile. This article is from the paper La Patrie *on May 14, 1874.*

A PERFECT DAY

The quintessential Renoir image is a summer's day, pretty girls, wholesome food, and a relaxed country setting. This imagery and the values it represents for today's audience have been adopted by the advertising industry.

Do you understand your own beauty? At our powder bar, the knowing consultant recognizes the beauty that is yours alone. Even as you watch, she heightens your best points...from the face powder she hand-blends for your coloring to the fulfillment of *all* your beauty needs. Made-to-order face powder, pressed in a compact, $2; or boxed loose, $1.50, $2.50. All plus tax. At favored department and speciality stores.

Charles of the Ritz

DURAND-RUEL

The art dealer Paul Durand-Ruel was influential in establishing Renoir's reputation. Durand-Ruel had been a long standing friend of Renoir and organized several solo exhibitions of his work, including a major retrospective of his work in 1892, and at his galleries in New York and the Grafton Galleries in London, in 1905.

A LASTING IMPRESSION

Renoir died in 1919, at the age of 78. On the morning of his death he asked for his paintbox and brushes despite being terribly ill with pneumonia. His son, Jean Renoir, wrote in his memoirs: *"He painted the anenomes which Nenette, our kind-hearted maid, had gone out and gathered for him. For several hours he identified himself with these flowers and forgot his pain. Then he motioned for someone to take his brush and said, 'I think I am beginning to understand something about it.' He died in the night."* Even before his death he had taken his place among the roll-call of great artists. His portrait of Madame Charpentier was acquired by the Louvre and he was fêted as his chair was wheeled through the galleries. His output was considerable; greater perhaps then any of his fellow Impressionist painters, having painted about 6,000 pictures. Today his works can be found in the major art galleries around the world, particularly in America because American collectors acquired his pictures when they were still unfashionable in Europe.

ALBERT BARNES

One of Renoir's greatest patrons was Albert Barnes, an American millionaire and art collector. Barnes created the Barnes Foundation in 1922, an educational foundation and museum containing many Impressionist paintings, as well as those by artists such as Manet and Matisse. The Foundation owns 180 paintings by Renoir, as well as 69 by Cézanne, and 60 by Matisse. Barnes believed that Renoir's art was richer than that of his Impressionist contemporaries because he built upon the Impressionist style to develop a more perceptive style of painting. The Barnes Foundation originally restricted access to its collection but now the works are made available for loan to exhibitions.

**LES COLLETTES &
RENOIR'S STUDIO**

Since 1960 Renoir's house at Cagnes-sur-Mer, Les Collettes, has been preserved by the Renoir Estate and the local government as a museum. It is surrounded by its 100-year-old olive grove and is a place of pilgrimage for Renoir students. Several works by the artist are still at Les Collettes. Another location that has been preserved in memory of the artist is the Fournaise Restaurant on Chatou island in the Seine, known locally as the Impressionist's island. It is possible today to have lunch on the same terrace made famous in Renoir's masterpiece *Luncheon of the Boating Party*.

DID YOU KNOW?
FASCINATING FACTS ABOUT THE ARTIST
AND THE TIMES IN WHICH HE WORKED

- Renoir proved to be so good at painting porcelain that he was given the task of painting profiles of Marie-Antoinette on to fine white cups.

- Five years after he had started working at the porcelain factory, machines for coloring ceramics were introduced so he switched from painting porcelain to decorating fans and screens.

- Renoir's son Jean recalled that his father always judged people by their hands. For instance, he once said: "Did you see that fellow, the way he tore open his packet of cigarettes? He's a scoundrel!"

- While employed as a porcelain painter, Renoir spent his lunchtimes in the Louvre, viewing the work of painters such as Delacroix, Boucher, and Fragonard. His son later said that his favorite work there was a sixteenth century sculpture called *The Fountain of the Innocents*

- When he left the porcelain painting factory, Renoir earned money painting murals for cafés.

- Renoir was one of the few Impressionists to use black paint. He called it the "queen of colors."

- When Renoir sat painting in the Forest of Fontainebleau, deer occasionally walked up to him. Sometimes he fed them bread, but then they would pester him for more, crowding round his easel and breathing down his neck.

- Renoir was not at all materialistic. He said all he needed were his two hands in his pockets. As if to prove this, on cold mornings, he used his watercolors and drawings to start a fire in his studio.

- In about 1865, Renoir met sixteen year old Lise Tréhot, whose dark features and rounded figure appealed to him. She became his favorite model and he painted her more than twenty times between 1865 and 1872, after which she married an architect and they never saw each other again.

- During the Franco-Prussian War of 1870–71, Renoir joined the army and spent the time training horses in the Pyrenees, far away from the fighting.

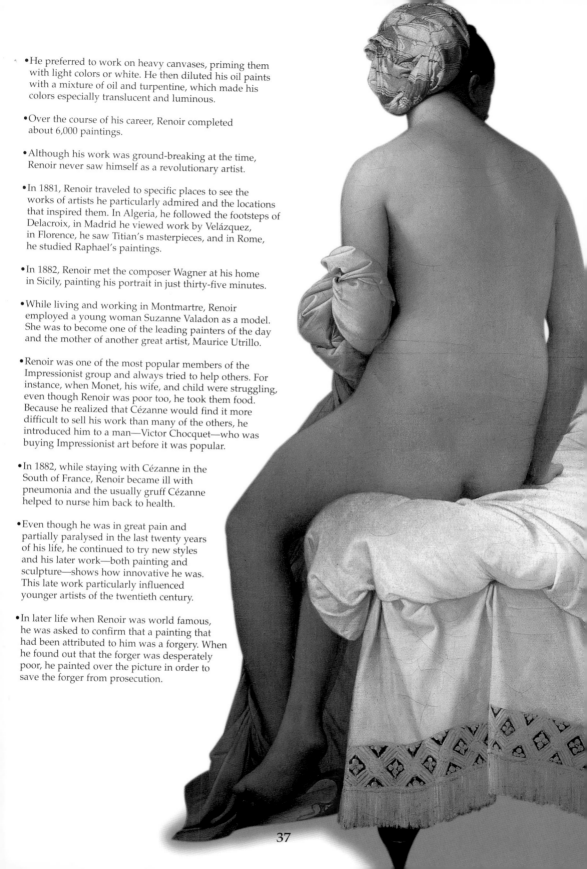

- He preferred to work on heavy canvases, priming them with light colors or white. He then diluted his oil paints with a mixture of oil and turpentine, which made his colors especially translucent and luminous.

- Over the course of his career, Renoir completed about 6,000 paintings.

- Although his work was ground-breaking at the time, Renoir never saw himself as a revolutionary artist.

- In 1881, Renoir traveled to specific places to see the works of artists he particularly admired and the locations that inspired them. In Algeria, he followed the footsteps of Delacroix, in Madrid he viewed work by Velázquez, in Florence, he saw Titian's masterpieces, and in Rome, he studied Raphael's paintings.

- In 1882, Renoir met the composer Wagner at his home in Sicily, painting his portrait in just thirty-five minutes.

- While living and working in Montmartre, Renoir employed a young woman Suzanne Valadon as a model. She was to become one of the leading painters of the day and the mother of another great artist, Maurice Utrillo.

- Renoir was one of the most popular members of the Impressionist group and always tried to help others. For instance, when Monet, his wife, and child were struggling, even though Renoir was poor too, he took them food. Because he realized that Cézanne would find it more difficult to sell his work than many of the others, he introduced him to a man—Victor Chocquet—who was buying Impressionist art before it was popular.

- In 1882, while staying with Cézanne in the South of France, Renoir became ill with pneumonia and the usually gruff Cézanne helped to nurse him back to health.

- Even though he was in great pain and partially paralysed in the last twenty years of his life, he continued to try new styles and his later work—both painting and sculpture—shows how innovative he was. This late work particularly influenced younger artists of the twentieth century.

- In later life when Renoir was world famous, he was asked to confirm that a painting that had been attributed to him was a forgery. When he found out that the forger was desperately poor, he painted over the picture in order to save the forger from prosecution.

SUMMARY TIMELINE OF
THE ARTIST & HIS CONTEMPORARIES

THE LIFE OF RENOIR

~1841~

Artists Berthe Morisot and Frédéric Bazille are born in the same year as Renoir

~1849~

Courbet paints *The Stone-Breakers*

~1851~

The New York Times is founded; in London The Great Exhibition is opened by Queen Victoria; Louis Napoleon, president of France, attempts to expand his power, dissolving the French National Assembly; the artist J. M. W. Turner dies

~1854~

In the year that Renoir begins his apprenticeship, Florence Nightingale and thirty-eight other nurses travel to help wounded soldiers fighting in the Crimean War

~1858~

After being made redundant

from porcelain painting, Renoir paints fans and screens; in Le Havre, Monet begins painting views in the open air

~1863~

The Salon des Refusés opens many artists' eyes to new artistic possibilities; Renoir and his friends paint in the Forest of Fontainebleau; Delacroix dies

~1865~

Abraham Lincoln is assassinated; the American Civil War ends and slavery is abolished; Renoir moves into Sisley's studio, he meets Lise and also Courbet

~1869~

Matisse is born; with Monet, Renoir paints *La Grenouillère*

~1870~

During the Franco-Prussian War, Renoir serves in Bordeaux; Paris is held under siege by the Germans; Renoir's friend Bazille is killed

~1873~

Renoir meets the art dealer Durand-Ruel and paints with Monet at Argenteuil; Levi Strauss & Co. begin manufacturing blue jeans, featuring patented copper rivets; rival cities Buda and

Pest unite to form the capital of Hungary

~1876~

Renoir visits the Moulin de la Galette, an open-air dancing establishment in Paris and exhibits fifteen works at the second Impressionist exhibition; Alexander Graham Bell invents the telephone

~1879~

Two of Renoir's portraits are exhibited at the Salon, he does not participate in the fourth Impressionist Exhibition; Edison demonstrates the electric light

~1882~

On his return from Sicily, Renoir visits Cézanne and catches pneumonia, he exhibits twenty-five works in the seventh Impressionist exhibition; Georges Braque and Edward Hopper are born; Charles Darwin and Dante Gabriel Rossetti die

~1889~
Renoir visits Cézanne; he refuses to participate in the Centennial Exhibition of French Art at the Exposition Universelle; the Eiffel Tower is constructed; George Eastman introduces the Kodak camera

~1890~
Renoir marries Aline; Van Gogh dies

~1893~
Morisot paints *Julie Manet and her greyhound Laertes*; Renoir spends more time in the South of France

~1898~
Marie Curie discovers radium and radioactivity; Tamara de Lempicka, Alexander Calder and René Magritte are born; Renoir has his first severe attack of arthritis; the artists Beardsley, Boudin and Moreau die

~1900~
Sigmund Freud, the founder of psychology and psychotherapy, publishes his ground-breaking book *The Interpretation of Dreams*; Renoir has a solo exhibition in Paris and sells most of the sixty-eight paintings displayed, he takes part in several successful exhibitions around Europe and is awarded the Legion d'Honneur

~1905~
Durand-Ruel organizes a huge Impressionist exhibition, including fifty-nine works by Renoir; at the Salon d'Automne, paintings by Matisse and other artists are labeled *Les Fauves*, meaning *Wild Beasts*; the artists Ashile Gorky and Willem de Kooning are born

~1907~
The Metropolitan Museum of Art buys Renoir's *Madame Charpentier and her Children* for 84,000 francs; Renoir buys Les Collettes, an estate at Cagnes and starts building a house there; Picasso paints the landmark work *Les Demoiselles d'Avignon*

~1910~
Renoir travels to Germany where he is participating in several exhibitions and there is a Renoir retrospective at the Venice Biennale

~1912~
An exhibition of forty-one works by Renoir opens in Munich; other works by him

appear in St. Petersburg, London, Mannheim, and various other places; the Titanic sinks on her maiden voyage

~1913~
Renoir takes up sculpture, employing twenty-three year old Richard Guino as his assistant and teacher; the Ford Motor Company introduces the first assembly line

~1915~
Aline dies aged fifty-six on her way home from visiting their wounded son in hospital; poison gas is first used on the Western Front; Einstein proposes his theory of relativity

~1918~
World War I ends and the Treaty of Versailles is signed; Renoir paints with a brush tied to his hand

~1919~
Renoir visits the Louvre in his wheelchair, where he sees the hanging of his *Portrait of Madame Charpentier and her Children*; he is promoted to Commander of the Legion of Honour—the highest accolade, in December he dies of pneumonia at the age of seventy-eight

WHAT DID HE SAY?

Here are some things that Renoir said:

• "An artist, under pain of oblivion, must have confidence in himself and listen only to his real master: Nature"

• "Shall I tell you what I think are the two qualities of a work of art? First, it must be the indescribable and second, it must be inimitable"

• "In painting, as in the other arts, there's not a single process, no matter how insignificant, which can be reasonably made into a formula. You come to nature with your theories and she knocks them all flat"

• "The work of art must seize you, wrap you up in itself, and carry you away. It is the means by which the artist conveys his passion."

• "The artist who uses the least of what is called imagination will be the greatest."

• "To my mind a picture should be something pleasant, cheerful, and pretty. Yes, pretty!"

• "A painting requires a little mystery, some vagueness, some fantasy. When you always make your meaning perfectly plain, you end up boring people."

• "Be a good craftsman. It won't stop you from being a genius."

• "Methods and techniques are not taught. One learns them oneself by searching."

• "Everything that I call grammar or primary notions of art can be summed up in one word: Irregularity."

• "I can't paint if it doesn't amuse me. And how can you be amused when you're wondering if what you're doing is making people grind their teeth?"

A WORK IN CLOSE-UP

Two girls sit on the terrace of the Restaurant Fournaise, just outside Paris. This is the same restaurant as in his painting *The Luncheon of the Boating Party*. The girls were not actually sisters, but two models Renoir used to create a charming image. He exhibited this at the seventh Impressionist exhibition of 1882. His free Impressionist brushwork and light colors were already changing to firmer drawing and more intense and vibrant colors.

It is spring, flowering plants are coming into bloom and there are glimpses of the River Seine through the trees.

The two girls wear bright, strong colors to contrast with the background.

The youngest girl's blue eyes echo the blue flowers in her hat.

Refined and smooth, Renoir painted the faces in his developing "dry" style, with no heavy shadows or dark tones, so the girls appear doll-like and extra pretty

The flowers and foliage are built up with patterns of different marks, including lines, dots, and dashes.

A glowing scarlet hat boldly stands out against the complementary green behind.

In the background, all is blurry to emphasize distance—a boat sails along the silvery river.

On the older girl's lap is a basket filled with balls of wool. The colors of the wool are dazzling, repeating the colors in the younger girl's hat and the older girl's corsage.

Two Sisters (on the Terrace),
oil on canvas, 1881, 39 x 37 in/100.5 x 81 cm,
the Art Institute of Chicago, Illinois, USA

WHERE TO SEE THIS ARTIST'S WORKS IN THE USA

There are many places in the USA to see Renoir's work. Here are some of them:

The Art Institute of Chicago,
Chicago, Illinois
(www.artic.edu)

The Detroit Institute of Arts,
Michigan, Illinois
(www.dia.org)

Fine Arts Museum of San Francisco,
San Francisco, California
(www.famsf.org)

The Guggenheim Museum,
New York City, New York
(www.guggenheim.org)

Hirshhorn Museum and Sculpture Garden,
Washington D.C.
(www.hirshhorn.si.edu)

J. Paul Getty Museum,
Los Angeles, California
(www.getty.edu)

The Metropolitan Museum,
New York City, New York
(www.metmuseum.org)

The Museum of Fine Arts,
Houston, Texas
(www.mfah.org)

The Museum of Fine Arts,
Boston, Massachusetts
(www.mfa.org)

The Museum of Modern Art,
New York City, New York
(www.moma.org)

National Gallery of Art,
Washington D.C.
(www.nga.gov)

The Barnes Foundation,
Merion, Pennsylvania
(www.barnesfoundation.org)

Norton Simon Museum,
Pasadena, California
(www.nortonsimon.org)

Brooklyn Museum,
New York City, New York
(www.brooklynmuseum.org)

Carnegie Museum of Art,
Pittsburgh, Pennsylvania
(www.cmoa.org)

Chrysler Museum of Art,
Norfolk, Virginia
(www.chrysler.org)

Clark Art Institute,
Williamstown,
Massachusetts
(www.clarkart.edu)

Corcoran Gallery of Art,
Washington D.C.
(www.corcoran.org)

Crocker Art Museum,
Sacramento, California
(www.crockerartmuseum.org)

Currier Museum of Art,
Manchester,
New Hampshire
(www.currier.org)

Dallas Museum of Art,
Dallas, Texas
(www.dm-art.org)

Dumbarton Oaks Research Library and Collection,
Washington D.C.
(museum.doaks.org)

The Frick Collection,
New York City, New York
(collections.frick.org)

Harvard University Art Museum,
Boston, Massachusetts
(www.artmuseums.harvard.edu)

Indianapolis Museum of Art,
Indianapolis, Indiana
(www.imamuseum.org)

Los Angeles County Museum of Art,
Los Angeles, California
(www.lacma.org)

Memorial Art Gallery of the University of Rochester,
New York
(magart.rochester.edu)

Minneapolis Institute of Arts,
Minneapolis, Minnesota
(www.artsmia.org)

Philadelphia Museum of Art,
Philadelphia, Pennsylvania
(www.philamuseum.org)

Portland Museum of Art,
Portland, Oregon
(www.portlandmuseum.org)

Saint Louis Art Museum,
St. Louis, Missouri
(stlouis.art.museum)

WHERE TO SEE THIS ARTIST'S WORKS IN THE REST OF THE WORLD

You can see works of art by Renoir in many places around the world, particularly in Europe. Here are some of the locations:

The Fitzwilliam Museum at the University of Cambridge,
Cambridge, England
(*www.fitzmuseum.cam.ac.uk*)

The State Hermitage Museum,
St. Petersburg, Russia
(*www.hermitagemuseum.org*)

The Louvre,
Paris, France
(*www.louvre.fr*)

Musée d'Orsay,
Paris, France
(*www.musee-orsay.fr*)

National Gallery of Canada,
Ottawa, Canada
(*www.gallery.ca*)

National Gallery,
London, England
(*www.nationalgallery.org.uk*)

Neue Pinakothek,
Munich, Germany
(*www.pinakothek.de*)

Städel Museum,
Frankfurt, Germany
(*www.staedelmuseum.de*)

Art Gallery of Ontario,
Toronto, Canada
(*www.ago.net*)

Art Collection of the Biblioteca Luis Ángel Arango,
Colombia, South America
(*www.lablaa.org*)

Art Gallery of Ontario,
Ontario, Canada
(*www.ago.net*)

Ashmolean Museum,
Oxford, England
(*www.ashmolean.org*)

Courtauld Institute of Art,
London, England
(*www.courtauld.ac.uk*)

E.G. Bührle Collection,
Zurich, Switzerland
(*www.buehrle.ch*)

Kunstmuseum Basel,
Basel, Switzerland
(*www.kunstmuseumbasel.ch*)

Manchester City Art Gallery,
Manchester, England
(*www.manchestergalleries.org*)

Musée de l'Orangerie,
Paris, France
(*www.musee-orangerie.fr*)

Musée des Beaux-Arts de Lyon,
Lyon, France
(www.mba-lyon.fr)

Musée des Beaux-Arts de Rouen,
Rouen, France
(*www.rouen-musees.com*)

Musée Marmottan,
Paris, France
(www.marmottan.com)

Museu Calouste Gulbenkian,
Lisbon, Portugal
(*museu.gulbenkian.pt*)

Museo Nacional de Bellas Artes,
Buenos Aires, Argentina
(*www.mnba.org.ar*)

National Museum,
Stockholm, Sweden
(*www.nationalmuseum.se*)

National Museum of Wales,
Cardiff, Wales
(*www.museumwales.ac.uk*)

New Carlsberg Glyptotek,
Copenhagen, Denmark
(*www.glyptoteket.dk*)

The Pushkin State Museum of Fine Arts,
Moscow, Russia
(*www.museum.ru*)

Oskar Reinhart Collection,
Winterthur, Switzerland
(*www.roemerholz.ch*)

Österreichische Galerie Belvedere,
Vienna, Austria
(*www.belvedere.at*)

The Ordrupgaard Collection,
Charlottenlund, Denmark
(*www.ordrupgaard.dk*)

Tate Modern,
London, England
(*www.tate.org*)

Rijksmuseum Twenthe,
Enschede, Netherlands
(*www.rijksmuseumtwenthe.nl*)

Thyssen-Bornemisza Museum,
Madrid, Spain
(*www.museothyssen.org*)

Wallraf-Richartz-Museum,
Cologne, Germany
(*www.museenkoeln.de*)

Yamagata Museum of Art,
Yamagata, Japan
(*www.yamagata-art-museum.or.jp*)

FURTHER READING & WEBSITES

BOOKS

Pierre-Auguste Renoir:
Paintings that Smile
(Smart about the Arts),
True Kelley,
Grosset & Dunlap, 2005

Color Your Own
Renoir Paintings
(Dover Pictorial Archives),
Marty Noble,
Dover Publications Inc, 2001

At the Time of Renoir
and the Impressionists
(Art around the World),
Antony Mason,
Franklin Watts, 2008

Pierre Auguste Renoir
(Getting to Know the World's
Greatest Artists),
Mike Venezia,
Franklin Watts, 2001

Renoir (Introduction to Art),
Peter Harrison,
Wayland, 2001

Renoir and Me,
Mila Boutan,
A&C Black, 2009

Pierre-Auguste Renoir
(Great Artists),
Adam G. Klein, Checkerboard
Books, 2006

Picture This! Activities and
Adventures in Impressionism
(Art Explorers),
Joyce Raimondo,
Watson-Guptill Publications
Inc, 2004

Start Exploring Masterpieces:
A Fact-filled Coloring Book,
Steven Zorn,
Running Press, 2000

Impressionists
(Young Reading (Series 3),
Rosie Dickins,
Usborne Publishing Ltd, 2009

Favourite Classic Artists,
Liz Gogerly,
Wayland, 2007

Impressionism
(Eyewitness Guides),
Jude Welton,
Dorling Kindersley, 2000

WEBSITES

www.ibiblio.org/wm/paint/
auth/renoir/

www.pierre-auguste-
renoir.org/

www.augusterenoir.org

www.theartgallery.com.au/
ArtEducation/greatartists/
Renoir/about

www.nga.gov/collection/
gallery/gg83/gg83-main1.html

www.nationalgallery.org.uk/
artists/pierre-auguste-renoir

www.wetcanvas.com/Museu
m/Artists/r/Pierre_Auguste_
Renoir/index.html

www.bc.edu/bc_org/avp/cas/
fnart/art/renoir.html

www.renoirgallery.com/
biography.asp

www.youtube.com/
watch?v=dn8eSVABMc0

www.renoirinc.com/
biography/artists/renoir.htm

www.nationalgallery.
org.uk/paintings/learn-
about-art/guide-to-
impressionism/guide-
to-impressionism

www.visual-arts-cork.com
/famous-artists/renoir.htm

robinurton.com/history/
impressionism.htm

renoir.chez.com/renoir3e.htm

www.phillipscollection.
org/collection/boating/
index.aspx

www.renoiruncovered.com/
painted-pleasure-renoir

GLOSSARY

Bas-relief—Shapes carved on surfaces that stand out from the background. Normally cast in bronze or built up in plaster, clay, or a similar material, high-relief *(alto-relievo)* has deep projections, compared with bas-relief *(basso-relievo)* which is shallow

Belle époque—A period from the late 19th century until the First World War, translated as "fine period," notable for its comfortable lifestyle free from major conflicts

Classicism—Ideas derived from the examples and styles of ancient Greece and Rome

Complementary colors – Colors opposite each other on the color wheel: red and green, blue and orange, and violet and yellow. When placed side by side, complementaries appear brighter than when they appear alone

Composition—In art, this refers to the combination or arrangement of elements in a picture

Gustave Courbet (1819-77) —An extremely influential artist who rejected idealization and Romanticism in favor of realism and was admired by the Impressionists

Louvre—The most famous national museum and art gallery in France. Originally a Parisian royal palace built around 1546, it has displayed art since 1793 and today attracts more visitors than any other museum in France

Pigment—Colored powder that is mixed with liquid to make paint. Usually made by grinding minerals or plants, the powder is added to oils for oil painting or mixed with other mediums to create different types of paint

Porcelain—A strong, translucent ceramic material mainly used for manufacturing fine crockery. It is made from kaolin (a type of clay) and a paste that includes substances such as soapstone and bone ash

Priming—Preparing a canvas for painting by applying an undercoat of paint

Rococo—This word derives from the French word *rocaille* (rock work) and describes a decorative style which became prominent in the early 18th century. It usually features small curves, rounded forms, and sometimes excessive ornamentation

Romanticism—An early 19th century art and literary movement concerned with the expression of feelings

46

INDEX

ACKNOWLEDGMENTS

Picture Credits t=top, b=bottom, c=center, l=left, r=right, OFC=outside front cover.

The Advertising Archives; 34tr. Archive Durand-Ruel; 29/29cb, 34bl. The Barnes Foundation; 35tr. Bridgeman Art Library; 12/13t, 19cr, 23bl, 24bl & 24tr, 27t, 29tl, 30l. Giraudon; 6/7t, 8tl, 8bl 8/9t, 10/11t, 10/11b, 11l, 12bl, 13cl & 13br, 14cb, 14/15t, 14/15b, 15tr, 16bl, 16/17t, 17cl, 17br, 18bl & 18/19t & 18/19cb& 19tr, 20bl, 20tl & 20/21t & 21cb & 21bl & 21br & 36ct, 22l & 22/23t & 23br, 24c 25tl, 25r, 26tl, 27bl, 28bl, 28tr, 30/31c, 31tr, 31bl & 31br, 32tl, 32/33cb, 33tr, 34br. Mairie de Paris © Photothèque des Musées de la Ville de Paris; 6bl. Musée d'Orsay, Paris/Giraudon/The Bridgeman Art Library; OFCb. Museum Folkwang, Essen/Giraudon/The Bridgeman Art Library; OFCt. National Gallery, London/ The Bridgeman Art Library OFC (main pic). National Gallery of Washington; 8/9b. Phillips Collection, Washington DC/The Bridgeman Art Library; OFCc. Réunion des Musées Nationaux © Photo RMN-Gérard Blot; 26/27cb. Union Centrale des Arts Decoratifs; 7r.

NOTE TO READERS

The website addresses are correct at the time of publishing. However, due to the ever-changing nature of the Internet, websites and content may change. Some websites can contain links that are unsuitable for children. The publisher is not responsible for changes in content or website addresses. We advise that Internet searches should be supervised by an adult.

48